AS A YOUNG BRIDE, a *Malihini* from "the States" as we called the mainland at the time (1936), I was terribly anxious to please my new Island husband. He was half Hawaiian and half New Englander. Big, handsome and athletic, and with an appreciation of good food that I was going to try to satisfy if it was the last thing I ever did. We were very much in love.

To the delight of my sister-in-law, I made a list, with her help, of all his favorite dishes.

Our first meal was poi and salted butter fish. I bought the poi at the old Poi Shop in Kapahulu. It was scooped from a huge crock in the large hands of the owner and placed in a bag.

The butter fish sounded easy. I thought all I had to do was fry it, which I did. After it was crisp I put it on a plate next to a bowl of lumpy poi, and generously poured the remaining drippings over the fish, never realizing I was serving my unsuspecting and uncomplaining husband pure brine!

That was forty years ago. A limited budget, four children and a hearty, healthy husband made me determine to learn to use Island products and other ethnic foods creatively.

CONTENTS

MEAT (Hawaiian, Japanese, Korean, Portuguese, Chinese) . Page 1–6
FOWL (Chinese, Island) . . . . Page 7
FISH (Hawaiian, Japanese, Samoan, Island) . . . . Page 8–11
DINNER IN A TI-LEAF . . . . Page 12–13
RICE (Chinese, Japanese, Island) . . . . Page 14–15
BREADS (Portuguese, Island) . . . . Page 16–20
ISLAND FRUITS . . . . Page 22–28
VEGETABLES, SOUPS, SALADS . . . . Page 30–39
DESSERTS, BEVERAGES . . . . Page 40–48
PARTY DISHES . . . . Page 49–56
WHAT NOT TO DO—ISLAND STYLE . . . . Page 58–59
"ISLANDIZING" YOUR MAINLAND DISH . . . . Page 60
ENTERTAINING HAWAIIAN STYLE . . . . Page 60
GLOSSARY OF ISLAND TERMS . . . . Page 61
TABLE SETTING FOR A LUAU . . . . Page 62
"ISLANDIZE" YOUR TABLE . . . . Page 62
NOTES . . . . Page 63

Photographs courtesy of Hawaii State Archives

Cover courtesy of Tropical Fruits Distributors of Hawaii, Inc., 429 Waiakamilo Road, Honolulu, HI 96817

MEAT

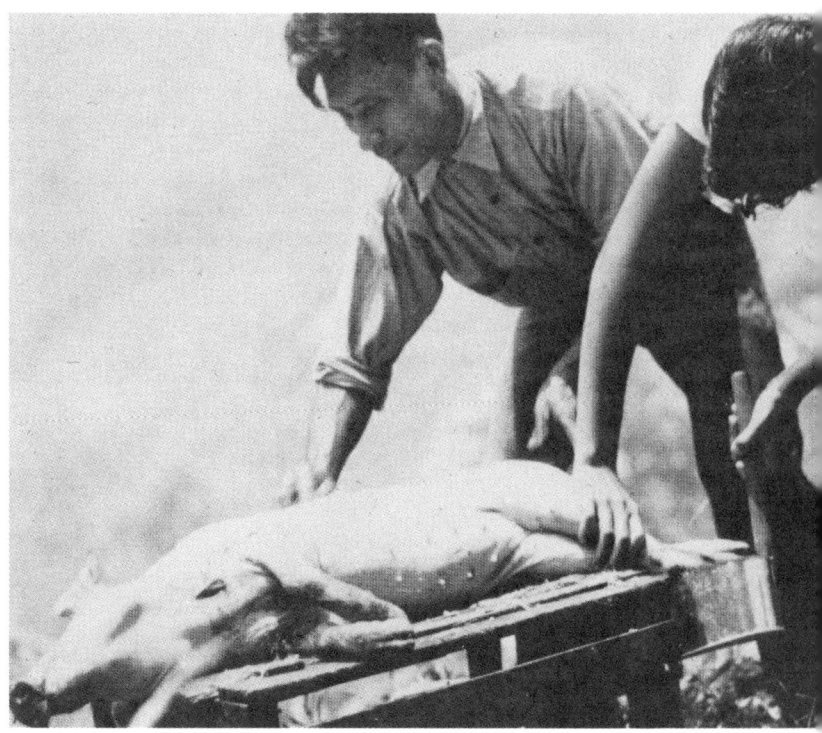

The traditional method of preparing Kalua pig for a luau consisted of cooking the pig in an underground oven called an "imu."

OVEN KALUA PORK ROAST (HAWAIIAN)

4 or 5 pound pork butt
3 Tblsp. Hawaiian salt
   (ice cream salt)
½ tsp. Ajinomoto (Accent)
¼ cup shoyu

1 clove garlic, crushed
1 tsp. Worcestershire Sauce
1 tsp. grated fresh ginger root
Liquid Smoke

    Marinate pork in the above mixture for two hours, brush lightly with liquid smoke.
    Place in a heavy roasting pan, lined with ti leaves (if available) or foil wrap securely in either and bake at 325 degrees until fork tender.

PARKER RANCH & THE PANIOLAS

Parker Ranch is located in Waimea on the northern tip of the Island of Hawaii. It was founded in 1847 by John Parker, a seaman. Today it is one of the largest ranches in the nation, second in size to the famed King Ranch in Texas. Parker Ranch covers 250,000 acres and runs 65,000 head of cattle.

Waimea is a colorful, lush country of rolling verdant hills, picturesque storybook houses and well kept flower and vegetable gardens. The climate is cool and crisp, guarded over by snow-capped Mauna Kea Mountain.

In 1793, cattle were first introduced to the Islands as a gift to King Kamehameha and they soon began to run wild. Horses were brought in 10 years later. A great percentage of our island beef today comes from Parker Ranch.

As the Hawaiians knew nothing about horsemanship, the King sent a chief to California to bring Spanish-American cowboys to teach them. The Hawaiians changed the word "Espanol" to "Paniola" and Hawaiian cowboys are known today as "Paniolas."

The Paniolas became adept at "cow-punching" and later won high awards at mainland and local rodeos for their skill. They are efficient, good-natured, hardy men, colorful in their broad-brimmed hats decorated with feathers or fresh flower leis.

TERIYAKI MEAT WITH NORI (JAPANESE)

1 lb. beef or chicken, sliced 2" by ⅛"
1 sheet nori (roasted black seaweed, found in Japanese stores)

MARINADE:
½ cup shoyu
1 tsp. grated ginger
1 clove garlic, grated
1 Tblsp. sake (rice wine) or mirin
3 Tblsp. sugar

Mix all ingredients well. Slice meat thin and allow to stand at least three hours or overnight in marinade.

Cut across the width of the seaweed to make strips ½ inch in width. Taking four or five strips of meat in one hand, fasten seaweed around the center of the meat strips. Deep fry until cooked and drain on absorbent paper.

BEEF STRIPS WITH MISO AE (SAUCE) (JAPANESE)

2 cups thin strips of sirloin
1 large onion, sliced
1 minced garlic bud

salt to taste
1 large package frozen oriental vegetables

Fry meat in hot peanut oil until pink is gone. Set aside. Add onion and garlic and cook briefly. Combine meat and onion and frozen vegetables (do not overcook, vegetables should be crisp). Pour miso sauce (below) over all and serve with hot rice.

SAUCE

1 Tblsp. sesame seeds, toasted
3 Tblsp. sugar
3 Tblsp. ground miso

3 Tblsp. shoyu
Dash of Ajinomoto

Grind or crush sesame seeds until fine. Add sugar, miso, and shoyu. Mix well.

PIPIKAULA (JERKED BEEF) (HAWAIIAN)

1½ lb. beef tenderloin
2 Tblsp. Hawaiian salt
½ cup shoyu
½ tsp. sugar
1 Tblsp. lemon juice

Pound the meat on both sides and cut it into pieces 4 in. long, 2 in. wide and ¾ in. thick. Sprinkle with the salt and let soak in the shoyu, sugar and lemon juice and let stand for 30 min. Keep it in the sun in a screened box for several days until well-dried. Broil or cook the meat in a frying pan over a hot fire until brown. Serve it hot.

KOREAN BEEF CUBES

1½ lbs. boneless beef sirloin, cut in cubes
¼ cup soy sauce
3 Tblsp. grated fresh ginger
3 tsp. sliced garlic
1½ tsp. sugar
Tops of 3 green onions, sliced
4 small, hot, red chilies, seeded and crushed
Salad oil
1½ Tblsp. soy sauce
1 Tblsp. toasted sesame seeds

Soak the beef cubes in the marinade of soy, ginger, garlic, sugar, onions and chilies for about half an hour, stirring once or twice. Drain the meat and brown it in the hot oil. Turn it out on a warm plate and sprinkle it with soy sauce and sesame seeds. Yield: 4 dozen cubes.

Pork is a favorite meat for any occasion and is generally cooked with wine or vinegar and highly spiced with chili peppers. **Carne de Vinha D'Alhos** or pickled pork must be marinated overnight to have that true tangy taste.

The fat was often skimmed off the cooked pork and used as a spread for bread.

CARNE DE VINHA D'ALHOS (PICKLED PORK) (PORTUGUESE)

4 or 5 pounds pork butt
1 cup vinegar
1½ cup water
¼ tsp. allspice
6 or more large cloves of garlic, crushed
2 or 3 Hawaiian peppers
5 bay leaves
1 tsp. Hawaiian salt or to taste

Cut pork butt into 1½ or 2 inch pieces, then put into a large bowl. Then add vinegar, water, allspice, garlic, Hawaiian pepper, bay leaves and salt. Mix well, cover and refrigerate for 2 days. Then cook pork in this liquid, covered, stirring off and on until cooked and brown.

It could also be cooked in another way (pan frying). For pan frying, drain all liquid, then fry in ungreased pan with cover, stirring until brown and cooked through on low fire.

BEEF PEKING (ISLAND STYLE)

2 Tblsp. peanut oil
1 tsp. minced, fresh ginger root
1 clove garlic, minced
½ lb. mushrooms, sliced into "T" shapes
14 to 16 snow pea pods, strings removed
1 lb. tenderloin steak, cut into thin slices
2 cups bean sprouts
1 carrot, julienne cut
2 to 3 stalks of celery, julienne cut
1 round onion, julienne cut
½ cup chicken consomme
1 Tblsp. cornstarch in 2 Tblsp. water
3 Tblsp. soy sauce
2 Tblsp. dry sherry
1 tsp. oyster sauce
Dash of MSG and salt

Heat the peanut oil in pan. Saute the ginger and garlic. Add the vegetables consisting of mushrooms, carrots, round onions, celery, bean sprouts and snow pea pods (Chinese Peas). Cook for 2–3 minutes. Push vegetables aside. Marinate beef with soy sauce, sherry, minced garlic and ginger. Saute the beef for 2–3 minutes. Then combine the vegetables with the beef and with the soy sauce, sherry, chicken consomme, and cornstarch mixture. Add dash of MSG and salt and oyster sauce too. Heat until sauce thickens. Remove to platter and garnish with parsley. Serves 4.

BROILED MEAT (KUN KOKI) (KOREAN)

1½ lb. round steak or 2 lbs. short ribs
¼ cup shoyu
3 Tblsp. sesame oil
3 Tblsp. toasted sesame seed
1 Tblsp. sugar
⅓ cup onion (finely chopped)
4 Tblsp. chopped green onions with tops
2 cloves garlic (finely chopped)
¼ tsp. black pepper

Cut steak into 3 by 4 inches and ⅓ inch thick or if ribs are used cut each rib apart. Pound the steak and score it with a knife. Combine the other ingredients with the meat, allowing it to stand for an hour or more. Broil over charcoal or pan broil in a skillet, turning often to brown. Serve hot with rice.

SUKIYAKI (JAPANESE)

1 lb. sirloin tip (chicken may also be used)
1 cup sliced round onion
½ cup sliced mushrooms
¾ cup sliced bamboo shoots
2 cups watercress, sliced in lengths of 1½ in.
1 cup green onion, 1½ in. in length
½ bundle long rice (wash and soak in hot water for 45 min.
½ block tofu, cubed
1 Tblsp. butter
4 tsp. sugar
½ cup shoyu
¼ tsp. Ajinomoto

Slice steak very thin. If chicken is used, bone it and slice it into strips. Heat skillet and add butter. Add a few slices of the round onion, stirring to prevent burning. Add meat and stir. When meat is about cooked, cover with sugar and shoyu. Let it come to a boil without stirring. Add bamboo shoots, rest of the round onion and mushrooms. Add greens last to avoid over-cooking. Add long rice and when transparent add tofu and Ajinomoto. Keep pushing things to one side as you add others. Serve hot, with rice.

FOWL

LYCHEE CHICKEN (CHINESE)

1 *fryer (about 3 lbs.)*
12 *water chestnuts*
1 *onion, chopped fine*
3 *cups oil*
1 *can lychees*

2 *Tblsp. cornstarch*
½ *tsp salt*
2 *Tblsp. shoyu*
2 *tsp. white wine*
2 *egg whites*

Simmer chicken, remove meat from the bones and chop fine. Add finely chopped water chestnuts (canned or fresh). Combine chicken, chestnuts and onion and mix well. Add the mixture of cornstarch, salt, shoyu, wine and beaten egg whites. After mixing, form into balls. Add to the hot oil and fry until golden brown. Drain and serve with additional lychees.

SWEET AND SOUR CHICKEN (ISLAND STYLE)

2 *whole medium chicken breasts, skinned, split and boned*
2 *small sweet red or green pepper*
2 *8¼ oz. can pineapple chunks*
4 *tsp. cornstarch*

4 *Tblsp. shoyu*
4 *Tblsp. dry sherry*
2 *Tblsp. honey*
2 *Tblsp. vinegar*
Dash *of pepper*
2 *Tblsp. cooking oil*
Hot *cooked rice*

Cut chicken into one-inch pieces. Cut red or green pepper into ¾-inch squares. Drain pineapple, reserving juice; set pineapple aside. In small bowl blend reserved pineapple juice and cornstarch. Stir in soy sauce, sherry, honey, vinegar, and pepper. Set mixture aside.

Preheat a large skillet or wok over high heat. Add cooking oil. Add red or green pepper. Cook and stir two minutes. Remove from skillet. (Add more cooking oil, if necessary.) Add chicken; cook and stir two more minutes. Stir soy mixture, blend into chicken. Cook and stir till thickened and bubbly. Add red or green pepper and pineapple. Cover and cook one minute. Serve over hot cooked rice.

As with other Oriental people who live in the Islands, the older generation of Chinese cling to their old food habits and customs, but the younger ones are more Americanized especially for the breakfast meal. However, at least one meal a day is typically Chinese.

FISH

Many people avoid buying a whole, fresh fish because they do not know how to select one. Checking for freshness is simple; look at both eyes and gills. The whites of the eyes should be clear and firm, not filmy or sunken. The gills should be red, for as the fish becomes older, the gills lose color, turning a faint pink.

Once you have purchased the fish you must decide how to cook it. Here is a brief list of fish especially good for certain preparations:

Baking—kumu, mahimahi, mullet, uhu, opakapaka and ulua.
Broiling—akule, kumu filets, moi, sea bass, mahi-mahi, moi or ulua slices.
Frying—ahi, sea bass, baby ulua (papio), or any other small fish.
Steaming—kumu, mullet, moi, onaga and opakapaka.

To help you translate those Hawaiian names, here are the English equivalents of popular fish:

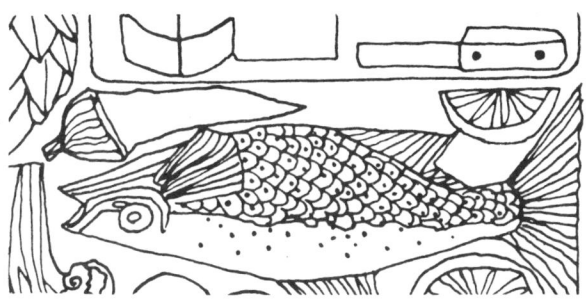

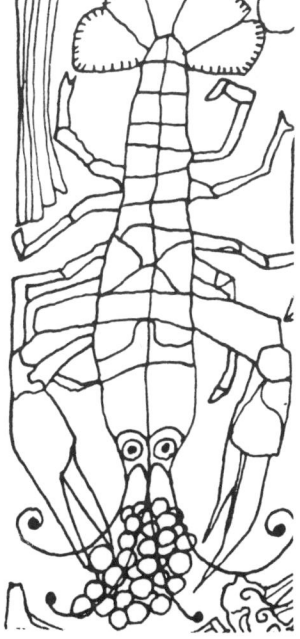

Ahi—yellow fin tuna
Aku—skipjack tuna
A'u—marlin
Kumu—goat fish
Mahimahi—dolphin family fish
Moi—thread fish

Onaga—red snapper
Ono—wahoo
Opakapaka—pink snapper
Opelo—mackerel-like fish
Uhu—parrot fish
Ulua—Jack Crevalle fish

LOMI SALMON (HAWAIIAN)
(Lomi means to massage or work with the fingers)

1 lb. salmon (those who know believe the belly is the best)	1 large onion (Maui preferred)
½ cup Hawaiian salt	3 green onions and tops chopped finely
6 tomatoes, peeled and chopped	

Cut the salmon in small pieces and cover with the Hawaiian salt. (If the salmon is salted, wash it and do not add salt.) Cover and chill. Rinse the salmon and place in a bowl, covering it with cold water and let it soak for about two hours. Taste it for suitable saltiness. Drain and pat dry and chop it coarse. Combine with the tomatoes and the onion and massage it all until well-mixed. Chill, covered for about three hours, serve with two or three ice cubes in the mixture.

Limu is a general Hawaiian name for all plants living under water, fresh or salt. The English word is seaweed, the Japanese word, *ogo*, and the Korean work, *miyuk*.

A familiar sight 40 years ago, along the shores at low tide, from Waikiki to Kahala and around Hilo Bay, was women, wearing broad-brimmed hats with their dresses tucked up between their legs, picking *limu* and also *opihi* (shell fish). It is important to know what *limu* is edible and what is not, as some, such as *limu-make-o-Hana*, are poisonous.

Most Hawaiians prefer to eat *limu* raw or lightly salted. A favorite Hawaiian method is simply to mix the cleaned *limu* with roasted, salted kukui nuts, chili peppers and seafood, such as opihi (shellfish).

Before *limu* can be prepared for consumption, it must be cleaned. Soaking the *limu* in water before cleaning helps to remove some of the debris, but bits of coral and sand must be picked out carefully by hand.

Most of the recipes call for the crunchy red *limu* found in supermarkets. Other varieties, if available, can be substituted.

SHRIMP TEMPURA (JAPANESE)

Wash and shell 1 lb. fresh shrimp, leaving the tails. Slit shrimp down center of back and open flat. Remove black vein. Place shrimp cut side down on board and score to prevent curling. Use dull side of knife and pound lightly.

BATTER

½ cup flour	⅛ Ajinomoto
½ cup corn starch	1 egg
⅛ tsp. salt	¾ cup water

Sift dry ingredients together; beat egg and water. Add to dry ingredients and mix well. For thin lacy batter, remove ½ cup batter. Add 2 Tblsp. water to it. The remaining portion is the thick batter for the shrimp. Heat oil to 375 degrees.

Dip finger in thin lacy batter and sprinkle over oil. Repeat several times until lacy network is formed. Dip shrimp in thick batter and place on lacy network when network is slightly brown. When tempura is golden brown, break network of batter and turn each shrimp. Drain on paper towels.

MAHIMAHI STEAKS with OYSTER STUFFING

6	medium sized oysters	2	tbs. melted butter or margarine
½	c. cracker crumbs		
¼	tsp. salt	6	fish steaks (sliced in two)
⅛	tsp. pepper	1	Tblsp. lemon juice
1	tsp. chopped parsley		butter or margarine for basting

Drain oysters and cut in pieces. Add crumbs, salt, pepper, parsley and melted butter. Mix well. Place half the fish slices on a greased baking dish, drizzle with lemon juice and sprinkle with a little salt and pepper. Spread with oyster stuffing and place remaining fish slices on top. Brush with melted butter. Bake ;in 350 degree oven for about 40 minutes, basting a time or two with more melted butter.

Serve with maitre d'hotel butter. Melt ½ cup butter or margarine. Stir in a tsp. of chopped parsley, ½ tsp. salt and the juice of a half a lemon. Serves 6.

STEAMED RED SNAPPER

- 2 lbs. Red Snapper (Opakapaka/Ehu)
- 1–2 large Ti leaves
- 4 whole peeled fresh tomatoes—chopped
- 1 c. liquid from tomatoes
- 1½ lemon
- 1–2 Tblsp. Hawaiian salt
- 2 cloves garlic—minced
- ½ round onion—chopped
- 1 large fresh mushroom—chopped
- ½ c. water chestnuts—chopped
- 3 oz. sesame oil
- 3 tbs. Oyster sauce
- ¾ c. White Wine
- ½ c. fish stock
- 2 butter pats
- 2 Tblsp. vegetable oil
- 1 Tblsp. Cornstarch—mixed with a little white wine to make a thin liquid
- ¼ c. Chinese parsley—coarsely chopped
- 2 drops Tabasco sauce

Make 2 slits in each side of the fish, rub half a lemon over the whole fish, rub rock salt over outsides and sprinkle inside of fish. Place on large Ti leaf and put in steamer for approximately 20–30 minutes, or until eyes pop out.

For sauce, saute in sauce pan: Vegetable oil, one pat butter, onions and mushrooms, until onions are clear. Add garlic and water chestnuts, let simmer for about 2 minutes. Add white wine and reduce liquid by one-half. Add salt and pepper to taste, tomatoes, tomato liquid and oyster sauce. Let simmer for 15–20 minutes, then add two drops of Tabasco, cornstarch mixture to thicken, swirl in one butter pat.

While sauce is simmering, heat sesame oil until it just begins to smoke. Ladle over done fish to add a crispy texture. Place fish on platter. Ladle sauce over fish, garnish with Chinese parsley and vanda orchid and parsley. Serves: 4–5 people.

I am often asked what to use in place of ti leaves which so many Island recipes call for. Romaine lettuce, fresh spinach or even the big outside leaves of cabbage may be used. They need to be slightly wilted in hot water first, to make them flexible enough to roll. Of course, nothing can match the unique flavor of ti leaves.

DINNER IN A TI-LEAF

8 ti leaves	Liquid Smoke
4 pork loins or chops	2 bananas
1 pkg. frozen leaf spinach	2 yams
1 pkg. frozen perch fillets	Hawaiian salt
1 large onion (optional)	

    Line heavy roasting pan with four of the de-veined and washed ti leaves.
    Place thawed but uncooked spinach leaves on ti leaves. Arrange pork and fish on top of spinach after lightly brushing each one with liquid smoke. Add sliced onions and sprinkle on Hawaiian salt (about 2 tsps.)
    Cover all with remaining ti leaves, tucking them under well.
    Wash and quarter yams and place on top of ti leaves, also the unpeeled bananas. Cover roaster and bake at 325 degrees for at least three hours, or until pork is well done. Serves 4.

ABURAGE NO NIKUZUME

4 tofu aburage	1 green onion, chopped
½ lb. ground pork	1 tsp. salt
½ lb. ground beef	1 tsp. shoyu
3 Tblsp. cornstarch	1 tsp. monosodium glutamate
1 egg, slightly beaten	

Dip aburage in hot water for three minutes and drain. Cut and open into a triangle. Mix the remaining ingredients and stuff the aburage.
Make a gravy with the following:

1 cup bouillon	3 Tblsp. sugar
½ cup shoyu	2 Tblsp. sake

Pour over stuffed aburage and simmer for about 30 minutes. Thicken gravy with cornstarch before serving. Serves 4.

TOFU MEAT LOAF (JAPANESE)

2 pounds lean ground beef	¼ cup minced green peppers
½ block tofu (bean curd)	½ cup dry bread crumbs
Pkg. onion soup mix (dry)	½ tsp. salt (remember soup mix is salty)
2 eggs	

Drain tofu and pat dry as possible in towel.

Mix all ingredients in large bowl after mashing tofu with a fork. Do not over handle meat mixture.

Place in a lightly oiled loaf pan. Bake at 325 degrees for one hour, add your favorite glaze and bake at 350 degrees for another half hour.

My family's favorite topping (glaze) is:

¼ cup shoyu	¼ cup brown sugar
1 tsp. prepared mustard	

Serves 6.

CHINESE RICE GRUEL WITH BEEF

1 cup rice	½ cup minced onions
7 cups water	2 Tblsp. oyster sauce
1 cup sliced or cubed tender beef	1 tsp. salt

Bring rice and water to a boil and simmer for about 30 minutes. Add onions and beef and continue to simmer for about 10 minutes. Add the oyster sauce and salt (and pepper, if desired). Serves 3.

RICE

Rice is the staple food of more than a half of the world's population. In some countries an invitation to share a meal is: "Come and eat rice." In many countries a girl is not considered fit for marriage until she has mastered the art of cooking a good bowl of rice. Rice is a symbol of fertility and we still practise the custom of throwing rice after newlyweds.

In China there is a custom of making a rice and fruit gruel at daybreak on the eighth day of the twelfth month and offering it to ancestors and friends as a gesture of thanksgiving. This is traditional to the Chinese as a turkey is to the American Thanksgiving.

Rice comes in many forms and types from cereal to rice wine and even rice oil.

A properly prepared dish of rice is the appropriate accompaniment for many dishes. Methods of cooking vary and may cause many disagreements. Some cooks believe it should be washed in several waters before cooking, others feel this washes away the added vitamins. An old time honored method is to allow the amount of water to rise above the level of the rice to the first of the knuckle of the fingers. All agree that the pot should be heavy and have a tight fitting cover and once the rice comes to a boil, the pot should be covered tightly, the heat turned very low and the rice is cooked by steam for at least half an hour. A well known Chinese cook gives the following method:

1½ cups rice   *1½ cups water*

Wash rice in cold water 4 times. Put in a Chinese steaming bowl, add water and steam 60 minutes. Rice will be dry and fluffy and serves 4.

RICE PANCAKES

1 cup cooked rice
2 Tblsp. finely minced onions
2 Tblsp. finely chopped green pepper
2 Tblsp. finely chopped celery
2 Tblsp. finely chopped water chestnuts
2 eggs, slightly beaten
Salt to taste
2 Tblsp. vegetable oil

Heat oil in a small skillet. Combine all other ingredients which have been mixed. Cook on low heat until eggs are set. Turn on to a heated platter, garnish with parsley and serve with Chinese Sauce.

CHINESE SAUCE: Blend 1½ cups water with 3 Tblsp. cornstarch, 1 Tblsp. soy sauce and 3 bouillon cubes. Cook over low heat until smooth and clear.

SWEET RICE (YAKSIK)

1 lb. mochi rice
1 lb. peeled chestnuts
½ lb. dates
⅛ lb. pine nuts
½ cup brown sugar
1 Tblsp. sesame or vegetable oil
2 Tblsp. shoyu
½ tsp. ground cinnamon

Wash and soak the rice in water for 1 hour. Drain and place the rice in a wire mesh basket or the top part of a metal steamer, lined with cheesecloth. Steam about 1½ hours or until the rice is soft. Cool and mix with the oil. Boil the sugar and shoyu 5 minutes and add to the rice. Cut the dates and chestnuts in halves and mix with the rice. Place the mixture in a steamer and steam for 2 or 3 hours. May be served either hot or cold and garnished with cinnamon and shelled pinenuts.

ISLAND-STYLE FRIED RICE

½ lb. rice
½ lb cooked ham, cut in strips
1 6 oz. can shrimp, drained
4 Tblsp. oil
3 Tblsp. soy sauce
4 green onions, chopped fine, green part also
5 eggs
Black pepper

Cook ham strips and shrimp in hot oil until lightly browned. Add rice and soy sauce, cook about 5 minutes, turning lightly, add the onion and pepper. Beat the eggs, pour over rice and cook until the eggs are set. Serves 4 or 5.

BREADS

A favorite bread is sweet bread (***masa savada*** or ***pao doce***). Formerly served only on special occasions, it is baked daily here in Hawaii. It is also sold at the airport where outgoing visitors can buy it. On holidays, small charms and coins and even whole cooked eggs are imbedded in the dough.

In Portugal, the Azores and Madeira, ***fornos*** or ovens are used to bake the ***masa savada***. The ***fornos*** in early Hawaii were large outdoor stone ovens made from bricks or black lava rocks. The risen ***masada*** was shaped and placed onto large banana leaf mats to be placed into the ***forno***. The temperature was tested by throwing a handful of flour into the opening. If the flour turned a delicate brown the ***forno*** was ***pronto***. In those early days ***fornos*** were quite common in the Pauoa and Punchbowl area.

The Portuguese were among the first Europeans to come to Hawaii beginning in 1878, and although they have adopted many of our Island foods and customs, they also cling quite closely to their homeland methods of serving food and table settings. A typical setting would be a centerpiece of fresh fruit, for example, a mound of grapes with green leaves, or a pyramid of lemons or other fruit in place of flowers. The dishes should be in bright colorful fiesta colors.

PORTUGUESE SWEET BREAD (PAO DOCE)

1 cup milk
2 pkgs. yeast
1¼ cups lukewarm water
14 cups flour
2½ tsp. salt
3 cups sugar
3½ Tblsp. butter
10 eggs

⅓ tsp. lemon extract
1 egg (for brushing top)

If desired; Wash ⅓ cup caraway seeds. Drain and boil them in 1 cup of water for 15 min. Cool and pour thru a strainer and add to the dough.

Bring milk to a boil, dissolve yeast in warm water. Sift and measure flour. Sift flour, salt and sugar, add the butter and mix. Add the slightly beaten eggs, lemon extract and yeast and mix well. Knead dough for 20 minutes, gradually adding milk as needed. Knead until no dough sticks to hands. Let rise in pan until double in bulk. Push down, then shape into round shapes and place in greased pans. Let rise until double in bulk. Brush tops with whole beaten egg. Bake at 350 degrees, one hour for bread and 20 minutes for rolls. Yield: 5 large round loaves.

Portuguese pastries, rich and high in calories, are generally reserved for special holidays. The important Catholic festivals which are celebrated by the Portuguese are incomplete without **filoses** or **malasadas** (fried doughnuts).

FILOSES or MALASADAS (SWEET DOUGHNUTS)

2 sticks cinnamon
½ cup milk
1 cake compressed yeast
2 Tblsp. lukewarm water
1¼ cups sugar
½ cup strained honey

½ tsp. salt
¼ cup butter
2¾ cups flour
3 eggs
4 cups salad oil
    (for deep frying)

    Heat the cinnamon in the milk. When it reaches the boiling point remove it from the fire, allow it to cool to lukewarm and remove the cinnamon. Moisten the yeast with the lukewarm water. Add the yeast, salt, sugar and melted butter to the warm milk. Stir in part of the flour, beating well to prevent lumps from forming. Add the beaten eggs and remaining flour to form a soft dough. Cover and place the dough in a warm place for 2 to 3 hours until it doubles in bulk. Drop by the tablespoon into deep fat heated 350 degrees. Fry until the pieces are evenly browned. Remove and drain them on unglazed paper. Roll the filoses in honey and sugar (or just sugar) and serve. Yields 24 doughnuts (1 doughnut–203 calories).

    In both Portugal and Hawaii, all food is put on the table and everyone serves themselves for simple everyday meals. For elaborate meals or on special occasions the European style of serving in courses is followed.

MANGO BREAD

2 cups mango slices (put in blender)
2 tsp. cinnamon
1½ cups sugar
¾ cup salad oil
⅔ cup chopped nuts

½ cup shredded coconut
    (if desired)
2 tsp. baking soda
2 cups all purpose flour
1 tsp. salt

    Mix and bake in a greased, floured loaf pan 1 hour and 15 min. at 350 degrees. Cool before slicing.

GOLDEN PAPAYA BREAD

½ cup butter or margarine
1 cup sugar
2 eggs
2 cups papaya pulp (sieved)

2 cups flour
1 tsp. baking soda
¾ cups macadamia (or other) nut bits

Cream the sugar and butter together and add eggs one at a time and beat. Sift dry ingredients and add to butter and egg mixture alternating with the papaya. Add the nuts. Bake in a loaf pan at 350 degrees for about an hour. Yields 1 loaf.

TROPICAL UNCHEESE CAKE

7 graham crackers or 1 cup crumbs
3 Tblsp. melted butter
1 block firm tofu, 20–24 oz., well drained
4 eggs
½ cup honey

2 Tblsp. lemon juice
1 tsp. grated lemon peel
¼ tsp. ground cinnamon
1 tsp. vanilla extract
2 medium bananas, ripe
1 8-oz. can crushed pineapple, well drained

Preheat oven to 350 degrees.

METAL BLADE: Place crackers, broken into pieces, in the work bowl and process to make fine crumbs. With machine running, pour in melted butter. Pulse on/off until blended.

Press crumbs into the bottom of a 9-inch springform pan. Bake 6 minutes. Cool on rack. Reduce oven temperature to 325 degrees.

METAL BLADE: Add tofu, broken into chunks, to the work bowl. Add eggs, honey, lemon juice, lemon peel, cinnamon and vanilla extract. Process until well mixed. Stop machine, remove work bowl cover and scrape down sides of the bowl. Add bananas, broken into chunks, and process until smooth. Scrape down sides of bowl, add pineapple. Pulse on/off only until mixed.

Pour into cooled crust. Bake about 1 hour or until center barely jiggles when pan is tapped. Cool on rack: Cover and refrigerate until well chilled. Serves 8.

BANANA BREAD

1½ cups all purpose flour
¾ cup sugar
1½ tsp. baking powder
¾ tsp. baking soda
½ tsp. salt

1 cup mashed bananas
2 Tblsp. lemon juice
1 egg
4 Tbsp. salad oil
¼ cup chopped macadamia or walnuts

Mix slightly, do not beat (except the egg). Pour into greased and floured loaf pan. Bake at 350 degrees for 1 hour.

PINEAPPLE UPSIDE DOWN CAKE
(Best when baked in a black cast-iron skillet)

1 pkg. cake mix (yellow, white or lemon)
1 large can pineapple slices
Small jar maraschino cherries

1 cup macadamia nut bits
1 block butter or margarine
1 cup dark brown sugar

In large skillet, melt the butter and combine it with the brown sugar. Sprinkle with the nuts. Arrange the pineapple slices on top of the mixture and place one cherry in the center of each. Allow to cool. Make the cake according to direction and pour the batter over the pineapple mixture. Bake at temperature indicated. When cake is baked place a large round platter or plate over it and turn it over. While doing this, be sure you do it over a table or large surface to catch the drips. May be served with whipped cream or vanilla ice-cream. Serves 8 or more.

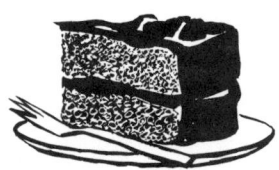

There were other uses for *limu* besides food in old Hawaii. When family dissentions arose a *Ho'oponopono* was traditionally held. This was a time when the family got together to "set things right." Wrongs and grievances were aired and discussed, forgiveness was asked and prayer was offered. Following this ceremony, family members ate a certain type of *limu* which had been cleaned and blanched. It was called *limu kala* which means to forgive.

Priests also employed *limu kala* in some of their rituals, one of which to purify those who had watched over and mourned a dead relative. Iolani Luahine, the famous hula dancer, wore neck and head leis made from *limu kala* during one of her performances.

Medicinally, *limu* is used to heal coral cuts. After being chewed well, *limu* makes an excellent poultice.

Before the kapu system was lifted in Hawaii in 1819, women were not allowed to eat certain foods, including pork, bananas, coconuts and many fish, so it was necessary and desirable to know where to find non-kapu foods such as invertebrates and algae. It has been estimated that about three ounces of a certain type, provides more than the necessary daily requirements of Vitamin A, riboflavin and Vitamin B12.

ISLAND FRUITS

Legend tells us that long ago all bananas bore their fruit on upright stems like the *fehi* (the mountain banana.) The lowland and mountain bananas fought. The lowlanders were defeated and from then on they have hung their heads in shame.

When Captain Cook first came to Hawaii, there were about 50 varieties of bananas which had been brought by natives on their migrations as one of their staple foods. Legends and superstitions about bananas abound. It has been called the "fruit of Paradise" and the "fruit of knowledge." In certain parts of Polynesia, young banana trees were used as flags of truce and the twisting of their leaves were believed to foretell cyclones.

BANANA MOUSSE

12 marshmallows
2 Tblsp. lemon juice
⅓ cup boiling water
⅓ cup mashed, ripe banana pulp
¾ cup whipping cream

Melt marshmallows in boiling water, then cool. Add banana pulp and lemon juice. When the mixture begins to set, fold in the whipped cream. Freeze in refrigerator trays. Yields six servings.

BANANA BUTTER
(Use as a pudding or cake filling)

1 cup ripe banana pulp	*2 Tblsp. butter*
1 cup sugar	*4 Tblsp. lemon juice*
1 egg	

Press banana through a sieve. Add butter, sugar, lemon juice and egg (slightly beaten). Cook over hot water about 5 minutes or until thick as custard. Yields 1½ cups.

When King Kalakaua, the last king of Hawaii, died in San Francisco his body was returned in a coffin to Hawaii. The body was removed to another coffin and a banana stalk was placed in the empty coffin buried in Kawaiahao churchyard. If this had not been done, the Hawaiians believed the coffin would have called for the death of a relative. The belief still lingers that to have a dream of a hole in the ground is the sign of an open grave and that to change the bad luck, the dreamer must plant some part of the banana.

BANANA COCONUT CUSTARD

2 cups milk
2 eggs
4 Tblsp. sugar
Dash of salt
¾ cup fresh grated coconut
1 cup sliced, very ripe bananas
¼ tsp. vanilla

Beat eggs slightly, add other ingredients. Pour into lightly buttered baking dish. Bake in slow oven (300 to 325 degrees) for about one hour or until inserted knife comes out clean. **Note:** As with other baked custards, place baking dish in a slightly larger flat pan half filled with hot water.

COCONUT

Among various foods, coconuts are very important to the Samoan people. The leaves are braided and used as baskets for carrying foods and as mats. The dry husk is used as fuel and the husk is also used for straining coconut cream. The soft coconut meat is fed to babies, and the mature meat is grated, squeezed and strained in coconut fibre to prepare coconut cream (*pe' epe'e*), which is used in numerous ways. Coconut milk and freshly grated coconut meat frozen can be purchased in our supermarkets today.

Coconut cream is used for a sauce in cooking and may have sea water or salt and water added if it is to be used with vegetables. Onions, lime juice, and water are added to coconut cream to prepare *miti*, a sauce in which cooked breadfruit, fish, and many other foods are dipped before they are eaten. Coconut cream is seasoned with lime leaves, lime or lemon juice before it is mixed with banana poi or mashed ripe papaya.

A substitute for fresh coconut cream may be prepared by soaking 1½ cups packaged coconut in 1 cup evaporated milk for 30 minutes, simmering for 10 minutes, cooling and straining with several thicknesses of cheesecloth. Then squeeze out as much liquid as possible from coconut.

TROPICAL FRUIT BARS

2 cups Bisquick (or other baking mix)
2 Tblsp. sugar
¼ cup firm margarine or butter
1 cup flaked coconut
2 cups candied fruit (cut up)
1 cup chopped dates
1 cup chopped macadamia nuts
1 can (14 oz.) sweetened condensed milk

Combine baking mix and sugar, cut in margarine or butter. Press mixture with floured hands in ungreased jelly roll pan and bake 10 minutes.

Sprinkle coconut over baked layer. Layer candied fruit and dates over coconut and then sprinkle nuts over fruit. Drizzle condensed milk over top. Bake until light golden brown, 25 to 30 minutes. Cool completely. Cut into bars. Yield: 70 bars.

PINEAPPLE

We are blessed here in Hawaii because we are able to obtain fresh pineapples almost the year around but many people get in a rut when it comes to serving them and limit them to fruit salads, or as a topping for ham or cake or as a beverage. There are many ways of serving pineapple ranging from chutney to meats.

Pineapple is a good source of sugar and calcium. In fact, it has more calcium than guava juice or Hawaiian oranges.

Spears of fresh pineapple are delicious and decorative in a tall glass of iced tea. Chutney pickles and jam can be made from pineapple, but do not attempt jelly as the fruit does not contain enough pectin.

PINEAPPLE PICKLES

3 cups white vinegar
3½ cups sugar
3 cups water
3 Tblsp. whole cloves

1 stick cinnamon
2 medium sized pineapples (about 12 cups)

After peeling the pineapples, cut them into sections about 1 in. thick, remove core. Combine with sugar, vinegar and water. Add the spices and boil slowly for 15 minutes. Boil gently in a covered pot for 1½ hours or until tender. Pour into hot sterile jars and seal. Yield 5 cups.

PAPAYA-PINEAPPLE POPSICLES

4 Tblsp. papaya pulp
6 Tblsp. crushed pineaple (drained)

1 Tblsp. sweetened orange juice or orange syrup

Mix together and freeze in popsicle molds. Yields 3.

SPICY PINEAPPLE

2 pineapples
1¾ cups sugar
¾ cup water
⅓ cup vinegar

12 whole cloves
1 piece stick cinnamon
1 tsp. grated fresh ginger root

Combine all ingredients except the pineapple. Bring it to the boiling point and add the pineapple which has been peeled and cubed. Cook on very low heat for about ½ hour. Pack in sterile bottles and seal.

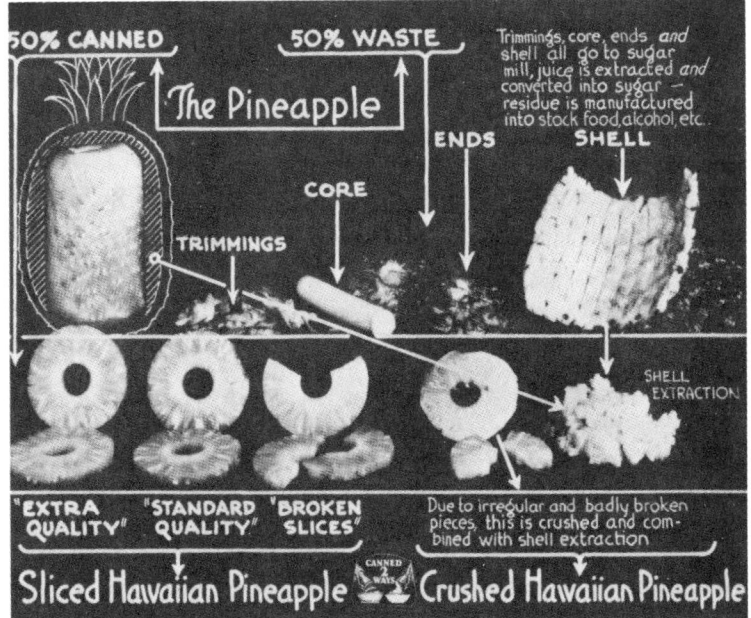

The anatomy of a pineapple.

A famous landmark, the Dole "pineapple" located in Hawaii's industrial airport area can be seen for miles.

MANGO

Kamaainas believe that a good mango crop insures a prosperous year. If this is true we are due for better days, as mango trees are groaning under their burden. When you are tired of eating those luscious, drippy golden jewels out of hand and are still eating last year's chutney, try Mango Kuchen. The combination of sour cream and mangos is tantalizingly different.

MANGO KUCHEN

½ cup butter or margarine, softened
1 pkg. yellow cake mix
½ cup flaked coconut
2½ cups sliced mangos (ripe but firm)

½ cup sugar
1 tsp. cinnamon
1 cup sour cream
1 egg

Heat oven to 350 degrees. Cut butter into dry cake mix until crumbly. Mix in coconut. Pat mixture lightly into ungreased oblong pan or cookie sheet 13 x 9 x 2 inches. Build up slight edges. Bake for 10 minutes (be very careful not to overbake, just until a very pale brown). Arrange mango slices on warm crust. Mix sugar and cinnamon and sprinkle over mangos. Blend sour cream and beaten egg and drizzle over mangos. Topping will not completely cover mangos. Bake about 20 minutes or until edges are light brown. (Again, do not over bake.) Serve warm. Serves 12 to 15.

PAPAYA

Papayas are gaining in popularity and availability throughout the world today. Among the best are those grown in Hawaii. They range in size from six inches around, which are called *solo* to large ones almost the size of a small watermelon, however, the *solo* variety are the sweetest. They are called *he'i* in Hawaiian and in other parts of the world *paw paw*. They contain vitamins A and C and calcium. The little black seeds are often eaten as an aid to digestion. A green papaya cut in half and rubbed over meat will act as a tenderizer. As a breakfast fruit it is delicious served with a wedge of lemon or lime and of course makes an excellent salad, combined with other fruits or cottage cheese. As a dessert, it may be topped with ice-cream. As a vegetable, the half green papaya may be baked like squash and served with butter and salt. As the flavor is a little bland, it is good combined with pineapple especially.

PAPAYA-SEED DRESSING

1 cup sugar
1 tsp. salt
1 tsp. dry mustard
1 cup red wine or rice vinegar

2 cups peanut oil (or other)
1 small onion, chopped fine
3 Tblsp. fresh papaya seeds

Put vinegar and dry ingredients in blender, gradually add the oil and onion. Add the papaya seeds and blend only until the seeds are the size of coarse ground pepper. Good on either green or fruit salads.

GREEN PAPAYA PICKLE (ACHARA PAPAYA)

1 medium-sized green papaya (3 pounds)
1½ teaspoons finely chopped fresh or preserved ginger root
2 to 3 cloves garlic, if desired
¾ cup vinegar
2 Tblsp. brown sugar
2½ tsp. salt
1 large carrot, if desired
1 medium-sized white radish, if desired

Finely shred or grate peeled papaya, carrot, and radish. Add 2½ tsp. salt and mix thoroughly. Let papaya mixture stand one day or overnight. Press out all the excess liquid and rinse the papaya in cold water several times. Mix finely chopped ginger, garlic, brown sugar and vinegar. Let stand 1 hour or longer. Strain the liquid and add to papaya. Adjust seasonings with more salt or sugar, if necessary. Place in a jar, cover and refrigerate for 2 or 3 days before serving. 18 servings—½ cup each.

PAPAYA AND GINGER MARMALADE

2 lemons, sliced thinly
1 tsp. grated fresh ginger root or 1 Tbsp. chopped candied ginger
4 cups water
4 cups sugar
8 cups chopped firm ripe papaya

Cook lemon in 2 cups water until transparent for about ½ hour. Boil the sugar, water (2 cups) and ginger to make a syrup. Add it to the other ingredients and boil at slow heat for 30 minutes. Pour into sterile glasses and seal with paraffin. Yield: 2 qts.

PAPAYA MOUSSE

16 large marshmallows
½ cup water
1 cup whipping cream
¾ Tblsp. lemon juice
2½ Tblsp. sugar
⅛ tsp. salt
1 cup ripe papaya pulp

Heat the marshmallows in the water until smooth. Add the sugar and cool, add lemon juice and papaya pulp (sieved). Cool until partially set.
Whip the cream, fold into the other mixture and freeze in icecube trays, or for a softer mousse, just chill.

A familiar sight in an earlier Hawaii was the Japanese woman, her child strapped to her back, gathering fresh fruits and vegetables.

VEGETABLES
SOUPS
SALADS

Buddhist priests devised many ways of using soybeans and their by-products. This accounts for the widespread use by the Japanese. Shoyu made from fermented soybeans, is indispensable in Oriental cooking where it takes the place of salt.

With the high price of meat, the soybean is becoming more popular as a source of protein. Different forms of soybean have been easily found in Hawaii because of its frequent use in Oriental cuisine, and have been among the vegetarian items generally stocked in health food stores. But now even Mainland supermarkets are beginning to carry tofu, the pressed block of soybean curd. A friend on a recent trip to the East Coast reported seeing fresh tofu in several supermarket chains in Connecticut.

Miso is another soybean product used almost daily in many Japanese homes. It is made from yellow soybeans mixed with fermented rice and salt, which is then ground and stored in wooden vats. Miso is used in soup or combined with meat, fish or vegetables.

Soybean curd, a white cheese-like protein pressed into cubes is called tofu when it is fresh and koyatofu or koridofu when dried. Tofu is a very versatile food, rich in highly digestible protein, low in calories and fat. This curd is quite perishable when not refrigerated. Tofu is delicious, whether added to meat and vegetable dishes or seasoned with shoyu and grated ginger.

Aburage is a triangular piece of tofu cut about three quarters of an inch thick and fried. It may be slit on one side and filled with a mixture of fish, cooked rice and vegetables.

TOFU TEMPURA

1 block tofu	1½ tsp. salt
3 Tblsp. toasted sesame seeds	½ cup finely chopped carrots
3 cooked shrimp, chopped	⅓ cup green beans, chopped
3 eggs	⅓ cup chopped burdock
2 Tblsp. sugar	(gobo)

Squeeze tofu in a cloth to remove excess water. Combine all ingredients and drop by teaspoon into hot oil. Drain and serve immediately. Serves 4 to 6.

BEAN SPROUTS AND AGE (FRIED TOFU)

2 pieces age (fried tofu)	¼ tsp. monosodium glutamate
1 pkg. bean sprouts	1 tsp. sesame seeds
1 tsp. salt	

Cut the age into strips and fry in hot, oiled skillet until brown. Add bean sprouts, salt and monosodium glutamate. Fry quickly until bean sprouts are just partially cooked and still crisp. Sprinkle with the sesame seeds just before serving. Serves 4.

Several thousand Chinese arrived in Hawaii and were established before large numbers of Japanese and Koreans came to the Islands, the majority coming from the southern part of China from villages near Canton. Most of the food and food customs show the influence of South China. The southerners emphasize flavor and texture of food and use less fat and less sweet dishes than those of the north. The best cooking is said to be found in Canton, Peking, Fukien and then Szechuan.

Their four basic foods are rice, soybeans, pork and vegetables. Because of undesirable conditions in which they are grown in China; they did not dare to use fresh vegetables raw but have learned to pickle, salt, blanch or to crystallize.

CONDIMENTS & ORIENTAL FOODS

Shoyu, prepared teriyaki sauce, sesame and peanut oil, preserved ginger, Ajinomoto, sushi mix, (rice wine) Mirin wine vinegar, oyster sauce, dried seaweed, Chinese 5 spice, water chestnuts, bamboo shoots, long rice, wun tun wrappers, lumpia wrappers, tofu, aburage, frozen coconut milk and syrup, mango and pineapple chutney, poha jam, guava jam and jelly, lychee nuts, abalone, lotus root, shrimp chips, kanten, azuki bean paste, sembei, sesame seeds, sesame candy, candied vegetables, fish cakes, squid, shark meat, fresh ginger, mountain apples, papaya, fresh pineapples, Maui onions, mangoes, soursop, taro, Chinese pea pod, dried fish, daikon, sashimi, gobo (burdock) just to mention a few.

Hawaiians eating poi.

CHINESE VEGETARIAN SPRING ROLLS

½ lb. bean sprouts
8 large mushrooms
3½ cups oil
2 stalks celery, slices
20 flour doilies 5/5 in.

3 Tbsp. shoyu
2 tsp. sherry
1 tsp. salt
2 tsp. cornstarch
4 Tblsp. water

Parboil the bean sprouts in boiling water for one second, remove and drain. Chop the mushrooms. Sauté the celery and bean sprouts in 2 Tblsp. oil for about a minute. Reheat the pan, add two more Tblsp. oil and sauté the pork and mushrooms for 2 minutes. Cool and spread 1½ Tblsp. of the mixture on each doily. Fold both edges about ½ in. moisten with cornstarch and water and roll. Heat 3 cups oil and deep fry until golden brown.

Between the years of 1907–1913, the first group of Filipinos to come to Hawaii were Tagalogs from Manila, then the Visayans. Today, island Filipinos are mainly Ilocanos from the northwestern section of the island of Luzon.

Because Filipinos have been in Hawaii a shorter time than other ethnic groups, they have clung to many of their own customs and mode of life. Through the years, however, they have adopted new foods and American methods of preparation. Pastries are becoming more popular.

Filipino foods frequently call for peas and a variety of beans. Pigeon peas, black-eyed peas and mungo beans, for example, are served in soup with pork or rice. Another popular preparation (adobo) uses a vinegar-garlic marinade for meats.

MUNGO BEAN SOUP (GUINISANG MUNGO)

1½ cups mungo beans or lentils
5 cups water
⅓ cup dried or fresh shrimp
⅔ cup sliced tomato
1 medium-sized clove garlic

½ cup finely sliced onion
1 Tblsp. fat
2½ tsp. salt
⅓ bunch watercress (4 oz.)

Wash and soak beans in 2 cups water for 4 hours. Rub beans between hands to remove skins. Discard skins but strain and save the liquid. Wash and soak shrimp in 1 cup water for 1 hour. Brown the mashed garlic in hot fat, then discard the garlic. Drain the shrimp but save the liquid. Fry the shrimp and onions for 1 to 2 minutes. Add tomatoes, beans and the liquid in which they were soaking, the shrimp water and salt. Simmer for 1 hour or until beans are soft, adding the remaining 2 cups of water during the cooking period.

Other greens may be substituted for the watercress. Lentils may be used if dried mungo beans are not available. Serves 8.

For entertaining, use an embroidered pina cloth or one made of organdy. The center piece is usually a three-tiered fruit plate.

SABULA DE VINHA (PICKLED ONIONS)

3 lbs. onions	1 Tbsp. Hawaiian salt
2 green peppers	(or ice-cream salt)
1½ cups cider vinegar	3 Hawaiian red peppers
1½ cups water	

Cut onions and green peppers into wedges. Combine vinegar, water, salt and Hawaiian peppers and add to onions and pepper. Cover; let stand 24 hours and then refrigerate.

Note: If you like this mixture hot, leave in the seeds of the red peppers.

PUDIM DE NOSES (WALNUT PUDDING)

½ lb. walnuts in shell or	1 cup sugar
¼ lb. shelled	½ to 1 tsp. cinnamon
5 eggs	Butter to grease mold

Grind or pound nut meats with the cinnamon to form a paste. Beat eggs and sugar; add nuts and cinnamon and mix thoroughly. Pour mixture into a well greased mold or 6 individual molds and set in a pan of hot water. Steam for 30 minutes or until done. Water should be kept at simmer during entire cooking time. It may also be placed in a pan of water in oven at 45 degrees for 30 minutes. Cool and unmold for serving. Serves 6.

Traditionally, the Filipino people do not do much baking. They instead rely on boiling, broiling, stewing and frying. Contrary to our rice-eating Islanders, Filipinos prefer sweet potatoes as a staple. In fact, a common sight in front of many Filipino homes is a lawn of sweet potato vines. Pumpkin and green squash vines, as well as many greens and edible flowers not found on our local markets are also popular vegetable garden plants.

ORIENTAL YAM FLUFF

1 large can yams, drained and mashed	½ cup brown sugar
	½ tsp. salt
1 flat can (8¼ oz.) crushed pineapple, well drained	3 Tblsp. melted butter
¾ cup quartered water chestnuts	¼ cup dry bread crumbs
	½ tsp. ground ginger

Blend yams, pineapple, water chestnuts, sugar, salt and two Tblsp. of the melted butter and spread in a flat baking dish. Combine the remaining butter and the bread crumbs and ginger and spread over the yam mixture. Bake at 350 degrees for about 40 min. Yields 4–6 servings.

Beans are also a popular and important part of the Portuguese diet and are often cooked without pre-soaking. They are cooked for a longer period and without stirring in order to keep the beans whole. The correct way to make the favorite and popular Portuguese bean soup is a controversial subject. Every cook claims he or she has the best and most authentic recipe. Our recipe is one of many but is considered true to the old country original and is delicious.

SOUPA DE FEIJAOS (BEAN SOUP)

2 cups kidney or pinto beans, canned or dried
1 soup bone with approx. 1 lb. meat on it
3 tsp. salt
Pepper
Oil for frying
1 clove garlic
1 medium onion, chopped
2 qts. water
¾ cup diced potatoes
¾ cup diced carrots
1½ cups shredded cabbage
2 cups watercress cut in 1 in. lengths

If dried beans are used, wash and soak overnight in 2 cups water. Cook until tender. Cut meat off of bone and sprinkle with salt and pepper. Fry meat in Dutch oven in a little oil with onion and garlic until brown. Add water and bring to a boil. Add beans and all the vegetables except 1 cup of the watercress. Simmer until meat is very tender and comes apart with a fork. Add remainder of watercress just before serving. Serves 8.

A touch of the past: A table set in the style of yesterday.

RICE SALAD

1 cup cold cooked rice
2 Tblsp. diced green pepper
½ onion, chopped

1 carrot, grated
1 Tblsp. parsley, chopped

Gently toss all ingredients with a fork. Add mayonnaise or a wine vinegar and oil dressing. Garnish with a chopped hard-cooked egg. Serves 3.

SUNSET SALAD (HAWAII)

1 cup seedless grapes
1 cup cubed pineapples
1 cup fresh or frozen coconut (thawed)

1 cup mandarin oranges
1 cup seeded lychees (canned)
1 cup miniature marshmallows
1 cup sour cream

Combine and chill overnight. Serves 8.

TROPICAL CRAB OR SHRIMP SALAD

2½ cups diced fresh pineapple
1½ cups shredded crab meat, or boiled baby shrimp

¾ cup mayonnaise
1½ Tblsp. catsup
1 tsp. Worcestershire Sauce

Serve the pineapple and crab or shrimp on crisp lettuce leaves. Add the catsup and Worcestershire Sauce to the mayonnaise and serve over the salad. If desired, add a tsp. of sweet pickle relish and ½ tsp. finely minced onion to mayonnaise. Serves 6.

TROPICAL COMPOTE

1 cup canned, seedless lychees, drained
1 cup cantaloupe balls
1 cup watermelon balls
1 cup tangerine slices

1 cup pineapple cubes, fresh or canned, drained
¼ cup maraschino cherries
Sprig of fresh mint
1 cup champagne

Pour champagne over fruit and let stand for about 20 minutes. Served chilled in small cups. Yield: 6–8 servings.

CHINESE SPINACH SALAD

1 Tblsp. white vinegar
1 Tblsp. soy sauce
¾ tsp. sugar
¼ tsp. ginger
3 Tblsp. peanut oil

1 green onion with top, chopped fine
6 cups torn spinach leaves
2 cups shredded iceberg lettuce
2 Tblsp. toasted sesame seed

In a salad bowl, mix vinegar, soy sauce, sugar and ginger. Add oil and onion. Add spinach, lettuce and sesame seed. Toss lightly. Serves 4 to 6.

TUNA CRUNCH SALAD

2 cans tuna
1 10-oz. can sliced water chestnuts
1 cup toasted slivered almonds
1½ cups yogurt
½ tsp. curry powder
1 Tblsp. soy sauce

1 Tblsp. lemon juice
1 cup slivered celery
½ cup seedless green grapes

Garnish: pineapple cubes and toasted almonds or macadamia nuts

Place tuna in a sieve and pour boiling water over it to wash the oil out. Chill before using. Blend yogurt, curry and soy sauce and add all other ingredients except the garnish. Chill well or overnight. Before serving, garnish. Serves 6.

GINGER-ORANGE SALAD DRESSING

1 bottle (8 oz.) Hawaiian-type salad dressing (Tropical)
½ cup orange juice
1 Tblsp. grated lemon or orange rind

2 Tblsp. chopped salted peanuts
1 Tblsp. finely chopped candied ginger

Pour contents into jar and shake well.

BANANA NUT SALAD

3 large or 6 small ripe bananas
¼ cup lemon juice

⅓ cup macadamia nut bits
Mayonnaise

Peel and cut bananas in half, lengthwise. Roll in lemon juice and then in nuts. Serve on lettuce with mayonnaise. Serves 6.

DESSERTS BEVERAGES

FLAMING DISHES

The story is told about King Henry the Eighth who presented his maitre de cuisine with a beautiful manor house because he was so pleased with a special dish the cook had created. Such generosity and appreciation is practically unheard of today, but a great meal and elegant dessert is of great value to connoisseurs of fine foods.

Adding wine to a dish, from soups to desserts, enhances the flavor and changes a simple meal into fine dining. The alcohol is burned off during the cooking process leaving an unusual and piquant flavor. The secret is not to overdo the amount. Two tablespoons of sake, sherry, burgundy or brandy, for example, added to a beef stew using one pound of meat is about the right amount, depending on your taste. But, be sure to add it toward the end of cooking.

Flaming entrees or desserts are not as difficult as they seem and are an exciting finish to the simplest meal.

BANANA CREPES WITH GUAVA SAUCE

CREPES:
- ½ cup sifted all-purpose flour
- 1 Tblsp. sugar
- ⅛ tsp. salt
- 2 eggs
- ¾ cup milk
- 1 Tblsp. butter (melted)

GUAVA SAUCE:
- ¼ cup (½ stick) butter
- ⅓ cup sugar
- 2 tsp. grated orange or lemon rind
- ⅓ cup guava juice (diluted if concentrated)
- 3 small bananas
- 2 Tblsp. rum

Place flour, salt, sugar, eggs and milk in a bowl. Beat until smooth with rotary beater. Beat in the melted butter. Set aside for 20 min.

Slowly heat a 7-inch skillet or crepe pan until a drop of water sizzles on it. (Butter skillet lightly for the first few crepes.) Pour 2 Tblsp. of batter for each crepe into heated pan. Rotate skillet quickly so the batter spreads evenly. Cook over medium heat until light brown, then turn and brown the other side. Place on a plate and after it cools fold it into quarters.

Combine butter, sugar, rind and guava juice in a large skillet and bring to boiling. Peel and quarter bananas. Heat in the skillet for about a minute. Add the crepes to reheat and spoon the sauce over. Heat the rum in a small pan; ignite it and pour it over the crepes. Serve 2 crepes and 2 pieces of banana for each person. Yields 6 servings.

BRANDY BLAZER

6 oz. *brandy*
2 Tblsp. *honey*
¼ cup *Kona coffee*
Lemon peel

For mixing, you need two heavy and deep mugs, about the 12 ounce capacity. Rinse them with boiling water. Pour honey and coffee into one mug and stir until honey is dissolved. Heat brandy in a saucepan until it is hot but not boiling. Pour into second mug. Light it. Pour the brandy carefully back and forth between the mugs. When the flames subside, pour the blazer into a thick cut glass goblet. Drop a twist of lemon in each drink. Serves 2.

BANANAS KILAUEA

½ *stick (2 oz.) unsalted butter*
⅓ *cup sugar*
1 *orange*
½ *lemon*
4 *ripe, firm, unblemished bananas*
¼ cup *orange liqueur*
¼ cup *white rum, dark Jamaican rum or bourbon whiskey*

This recipe is for table top cooking. Begin, however, with the following preliminaries in the kitchen:

Cream butter with 4 tablespoons of sugar. Grate in the peel of the orange, then, by droplets, beat in as much of its strained juice as the butter will absorb without separating. Turn this orange butter into an attractive bowl, pour remaining orange juice into a small pitcher and halve the lemon. Arrange the remaining ingredients on a tray, along with a cutting board for bananas, a sharp knife and sharp pronged fork to halve them, a long handled spoon and fork for cooking, and a spatula for serving.

Cook as follows at the table:

Place orange butter in a chafing dish and turn the heat to high. Pour in orange juice and dramatically squeeze the juice of the half lemon by piercing it with your fork and squeezing from high above the dish. While the butter, sugar and juices are boiling into a thick syrup, cut bananas in half lengthwise, being very careful not to break them.

When syrup is thick and almost a caramel, carefully transfer bananas to the pan using a fork to lift them from their skins. Baste bananas with the syrup in the pan, lower heat and pour in the orange liqueur. Continue basting until well heated and slightly softened.

Now, the flaming finish.

As soon as the bananas are done, sprinkle with a teaspoon or two of sugar. Pour in the rum or whiskey, tilt the pan into the flame (or flame with a match) and spoon the burning liquid over the bananas until the flames subside. Serves 4.

MY THRIFTY little Scots mother, used to say: "Anyone with average intelligence and a good recipe book can cook, but it takes a good cook to make something out of nothing." This makes cooking a challenge and takes a great deal of imagination.

During a brief nap one afternoon, my friend dreamed up a great dessert made with tofu (bean curd). It sounds crazy but she got up and while still in the mood, concocted the following with a half block of tofu left over from the night before. She calls it:

ORIENTAL DREAM

2 envelopes unflavord gelatin
½ cup cold milk
1 cup milk, heated to a full boil
2 eggs
⅔ cup sugar

⅛ tsp. salt
2 tsps. vanilla
½ block tofu (bean curd)
1 cup ice cubes
2 or 3 drops red food coloring (for a delicate tint)

Wrap tofu in a clean terry cloth and let stand for about an hour or until the moisture is absorbed.

Dissolve gelatin in the ½ cup cold milk, until granules are moistened.

Pour the above in a blender, add boiling milk, cover and blend at low speed until gelatin dissolves (about 2 min.). Stop blender.

Add eggs, sugar, salt, vanilla, food coloring and crumbled tofu. Turn on to high speed. Remove cover and with blender still running, add ice cubes, one at a time until melted.

Serve in parfait glasses and garnish with a whole strawberry and a sprig of mint. Serves 6.

MAUNAKEA SNOWBALLS

1 cup butter or margarine
½ cup sifted confectioners sugar
1 tsp. vanilla
¼ tsp. salt

2¼ cups sifted all purpose flour
1 cup uncooked oats
½ cup chopped macadamia nuts

Blend butter, sugar and vanilla until light and fluffy. Add salt and flour; mix well. Stir in oats and nuts. Form into small 1 inch balls. Place on unbuttered cookie sheet. Bake in 400 degree oven 10–12 minutes. Remove from cookie sheet and roll in additional confectioners sugar, colored sprinkles, chocolate shot, silver drops or chopped nuts. Place on racks to cool. Makes about 8 dozen snowballs.

HAUPIA

3 Tblsp. corn starch
3 Tblsp. sugar
⅛ tsp. salt
2 cups coconut milk

Combine dry ingredients. Add half of the coconut milk and blend to a smooth paste. Heat the remaining milk over low heat, add the cornstarch mixture and cook until smooth and thick (stirring constantly). Pour into a pan and cool. Cut into 6 squares. Serve on ti leaf squares.

COCONUT MILK: Pour 1½ cups boiling milk over the same amount of fresh grated coconut. Let stand for 20 minutes and strain, pressing down with a spoon in a sieve. Frozen coconut milk may be bought in a super market, follow directions for Haupia on the can.

EASY HAUPIA

1 small can frozen coconut milk
Cornstarch and sugar (as directed)
1 can cherry pie filling
1 prepared graham cracker crust

Cook the haupia as directed on the frozen coconut can. Cool slightly and fill the crust. Top with cherry pie filling and refrigerate.

ORIENTAL TREASURE COOKIES (CHINESE)

COOKIE DOUGH
1⅓ cups flour
1½ tsp. baking powder
½ tsp. baking soda
½ cup firmly packed brown sugar
⅓ cup sugar
½ cup shortening
1 egg
1 Tblsp. soy sauce
½ tsp. almond extract

ALMOND TOPPING
½ cup slivered almonds
2 tsp. sugar
1 tsp. soy sauce

Preheat oven to 350 degrees. Sift together flour, baking powder and baking soda. In large bowl, combine with remaining cookie dough ingredients. Blend well with a mixer. Shape into balls, using a rounded teaspoon for each. In another bowl, combine all ingredients for almond topping. Dip the top of each cookie into almond mixture. Place on ungreased cookie sheet. Bake at 350 degrees for 12 to 15 minutes. Makes 48 cookies.

CHINESE PRESERVED SEED

A confection, Chinese in origin, which is extremely popular with Islanders is the preserved seed. It has many varieties including sweet, sweet-sour, salty, cracked or whole. It is made from the seeds of prunes, plums, mango, apricot, lemon and even star fruit.

The first Chinese immigrants to arrive in Hawaii brought the seeds with them. That was a long time ago, but seeds are still a delectable treat to the initiated. Old-timers consider a li hing mui in a cup of hot tea a sure cure for many ailments.

The exotic seeds take a bit of getting used to, but quickly become a passion. The food generally requested by Island students attending school on the Mainland is preserved seeds.

Visitors are amazed and curious when they first see the myriad huge glass jars in the crack seed stores. One of the most popular stores is at Ala Moana Shopping Center where they carry about 100 different preserved seeds as well as other tasty, tangy morsels, including dried cuttlefish, coconut chips and red coconut balls. The generous people who work there offer samples also. Yick Lung Company has 24 different types of seeds and the grocery shops on Maunakea Street are favorites of old-timers.

CANTON MUI

4   12-ounce pkgs. pitted prunes
3   ounces preserved lemon peel (slice thinly)
2-ounce pkg. seedless li hing mui (buy at a seed shop)
½ lb. light brown sugar

1½ Tblsp. Hawaiian salt
1½ Tblsp. brandy
½ tsp. Chinese five spice
5   whole cloves
¾ cup fresh lemon juice

Place all ingredients in a large glass jar. Toss well, cover and let stand for four days or more. Toss and mix two times a day. Yield: ½ gallon.

PRESERVED FRUIT

1   box dried fruit (apricots, prunes or half of each)
2   Tblsp. sugar

2   Tblsp. salt
Juice of one lemon

Put all ingredients in a large glass jar and shake well. Place in the sun for four days.

BEVERAGES—ISLAND STYLE

Don't approach a Mai Tai with too much enthusiasm as this is a potent drink. Sip it slowly through a straw and don't make any important decisions over it.

MAI TAI

Shaved or crushed ice
1 lime (juice)
½ tsp. Rock Candy Syrup
   (Trader Vic's)
½ tsp. Orange Curacao

2½ oz. light rum
½ oz. dark rum
Mint
Pineapple spear

Fill a 14 oz. glass with ice. Stir in lime juice, syrup, Curacao and light rum. Float dark rum on top. Garnish with pineapple and a sprig of mint. Decorate with a vanda orchid. Serve with a straw. May be served in a scooped out pineapple shell.

STRAWBERRY BANANA DRINK

1 large, very ripe banana
¾ cup milk
6 ripe strawberries
¼ tsp. vanilla

⅛ tsp. salt
1 tsp. powdered sugar
3 ice cubes

Combine all ingredients in a blender until well mixed. Serve immediately in an icy glass. Yields one serving.

VARIATION: For a nourishing breakfast drink, add ¼ cup orange juice and 1 raw egg instead of strawberries.

As to beverages, If you are serving punch, a thoughtful hostess will serve both alcoholic and non-alcoholic. At a reception I once attended at Washington Place, a bunch of purple grapes was fastened to the edge of the punchbowl containing just the fruit juice. Iced coffee on a warm day can be served in a crystal bowl with dollops of vanilla ice cream floating in it. Don't be caught without plenty of ice; you can't have too much.

One of the finest coffees in the world grows right here in Kona. The first coffee plants were brought to Hawaii in 1823. Planted in Manoa Valley where the University of Hawaii now stands, they did not do well. In 1828 the Rev. Samuel Ruggles took the shrub to Kona. At first it was used only as ornamental decoration, but in 1850 serious efforts to produce a coffee crop began. The Kona areas have all the conditions necessary for growing fine coffee—volcanic soil, ample rainfall and natural shade cover from the great mountains.

Coffee was enjoyed in the Arab world for years before being introduced into Europe. Legend tells how the West began drinking it... Rumors told of a "devil's potion" drunk by the Arabs. This news made the Pope curious enough to taste it. The drink, the Pope decreed, was too good for the infidels alone, and thus he baptized it and made coffee Christian.

Today, of course, coffee is drunk around the world. But according to an ancient Arab manuscript, coffee should only be drunk without cream: "He that would drink it for liveliness sake and to dispel slothfulness, let him use sweetmeates with it and the ovle of pistaccioes and butter. Some drink it with milk, but it is an error and such as may bring in the danger of leprosy."

KONA COFFEE–CALIFORNIA STYLE

For each serving, pour 2 Tblsp. brandy into a coffee mug. Fill cup ⅔ full with hot strong coffee. Add one scoop of chocolate ice cream. Serve at once.

Instead of ice cream, place 1 or 2 Tblsp. of ready-to-spread chocolate frosting in the cup, fill with hot coffee and stir until blended. Top with whipped cream.

In my own home I have a collection of over 100 coffee mugs hanging in the kitchen, every one with a story. Inviting guests to choose their own cups starts the fun and puts them at their ease.

Besides being used as a beverage, coffee can be added to many different recipes.

MOCHA SPONGE

1 Tblsp. gelatin
¼ cup cold water
1½ cup Kona coffee
¾ cup sugar
½ cup milk

3 eggs (separated)
½ tsp. vanilla
⅛ tsp salt
Whipped cream

Soak gelatin in water, then dissolve in hot coffee. Add ⅓ cup sugar and the milk. Cook and stir these ingredients over a low flame until hot. Do not allow to boil. In a separate bowl, beat egg yolks and add remaining sugar. Pour part of the hot liquid over them.
Return to pan and cook for 2 minutes to permit the yolks to thicken slightly. Do not boil. Cool ingredients until thick. Add the vanilla. Whip with a wire whip until fluffy. Whip egg whites and salt until stiff. Fold into the gelatin mixture and pour into a wet mold. Chill thoroughly. Unmold and serve with cream (whipped or rich coffee cream). Serves 6.

Kona is now the center of coffee production in Hawaii. Like the regional designations given to French wines, the term "Kona coffee" is restricted by law. Only coffee produced in Kona can be so labelled. Known as the "aristocrat of coffees," Kona coffee is distinguished for its great strength, delicious aroma and fine flavor.

IRISH KONA COFFEE PIE with MACADAMIA CRUST

- 1 8 inch baked pie crust with ½ cup macadamia nut bits added
- 1 pkg. unflavored gelatin
- ¾ cup sugar
- 2 Tblsp. instant Kona coffee
- 1 cup milk
- 2 eggs separated
- 2 Tblsp. whiskey or ¼ tsp. brandy or rum flavoring
- 1 cup whipping cream
- 1 milk chocolate bar (softened to room temperature)

Make your favorite pie crust, adding the nut bits. Be sure to make an extra high rim. Bake and cool.

In heavy saucepan, combine the sugar, coffee and gelatin, gradually stirring in the milk. Cook over low heat, stirring constantly until ingredients are dissolved (5–10 min.).

Beat egg-yolks and stir half the hot mixture into the egg-yolks, return all to the saucepan and continue to cook, stirring constantly until slightly thick (3–5 mon.).

Chill until thick and syrupy. Add whiskey or flavoring and beat until frothy.

In a clean bowl, beat egg-whites until firm but moist peaks form and fold into the gelatin mixture.

Whip the cream in the same bowl and fold it into the filling.

Fill the pie shell and chill for about 2 hours. Garnish with chocolate curls made by drawing a vegetable peeler across candy bar.

COFFEE TARTS

- 6 baked tart shells
- 2 cups Kona coffee
- 1 cup evaporated milk
- 6 Tblsp. sifted flour
- ⅔ cup sugar
- ¼ tsp. salt
- 2 eggs or 5 egg yolks
- 2 Tblsp. butter
- 1 tsp. vanilla or 2 tsp. rum flavoring
- Whipped cream
- Crushed macadamia nut brittle

Combine milk, flour, sugar and salt with hot coffee. Stir until smooth. Cook over hot water until mixture thickens (about 20 minutes). Pour part of it over beaten eggs. Return this to the double boiler, stir and cook for 3 or 4 minutes to permit the eggs to thicken slightly. Add the butter and cool. Next add the flavoring. Fill tart shells; chill. Before serving, top with whipped cream and nut brittle.

PARTY DISHES

One of the first Hawaiian words that every newcomer learns is *pupu* or hors d'oeuvre. But few people, including long-time residents, know that the word originally referred to the fish, chicken or banana served to take the biting aftertaste from the potent kava drink.

Today, of course, *pupu* refers to many different kinds of relishes or finger foods. In Hawaii a *pupu* party can be a sampling of numerous ethnic foods served in bite-size portions.

WATER CHESTNUT APPETIZERS

1 can (5 oz.) water chestnuts, drained
¼ cup soy sauce
¼ cup sugar
4 slices bacon, cut in half crosswise and lengthwise

Marinate the chestnuts in soy sauce for 30 minutes. Roll each nut in sugar, then wrap with a strip of bacon and secure with a pick. Place them on a rack on the broiler. Bake in a hot oven (400 degrees) for about 20 minutes. Drain on paper towels. These may be made in the morning and reheated in a moderate oven for about 5 minutes. Yield: 16 appetizers.

Note: For Japanese rumaki, add ¾ lb. chicken livers, washed, drained and cut in half and wrap them around the water chestnut before wrapping with baoon.

CHICKEN PUPU CHUNKS

2 whole fryer-chicken breasts
1 egg, beaten
⅓ cup water
½ cup flour
2 tsp. sesame seed
½ tsp. salt
2 cups cooking oil

Skin (and debone if necessary) chicken breasts and cut into 1 inch square pieces. Mix egg and water, add flour, sesame seed and salt and stir to smooth batter. Fill heavy saucepan or deep fryer ⅓ full with cooking oil. Dip chunks in batter and fry four or five at a time until golden brown, about five minutes, and fork tender. (Do not add too many at one time as you want each to be separate and retain its chunky look.) Serve with a mixture of shoyu and Chinese mustard; add a small amount of pineapple juice for a different, tangy taste.

COCONUT CANAPES (SAMOAN)

8 oz. cream cheese
3 Tblsp. chopped, pineapple chutney
3 Tblsp. candied ginger (chopped)
¼ cup grated fresh coconut
½ tsp. curry powder
3 lengthwise slices white bread (cut from a whole, unsliced loaf)
Butter
Parsley (chopped) for garnish

Soften the cream cheese and blend in the next four ingredients. Trim crusts from the bread and toast it. Butter the toast and spread with the mixture, sprinkle chopped parsley on top. Cut into desired shapes. Yield: 30 canapes.

WATER CHESTNUT AND PINEAPPLE ROLL UPS

Bacon
Water chestnuts (canned)
Pineapple chunks

Cut bacon slices in thirds. Slice water chestnuts and drain pineapple chunks. Wrap a bacon third around a chunk of pineapple and a slice of chestnut. Secure with a toothpick. Broil, turning once or twice, until bacon is crisp. Drain on paper towel. Put on rack in shallow baking pan, and reheat in preheated 350 degree oven about five minutes just before serving.

MEAT STICKS

1 lb. round steak, about 1 inch thick
1 clove garlic, thinly sliced
Fresh ginger, about 1 inch piece, thinly sliced
⅓ cup soy sauce
2 Tblsp. sherry
3 tsp. sugar

Slice meat very thin. Combine remaining ingredients and mix well. Marinate meat in sauce for about ½ hour. Thread on bamboo sticks or skewers and broil over hot coals or in broiler. Makes about 20 meat sticks.

SATAN'S DIP

1 cup dairy sour cream
1 cup cottage cheese (small curd)
½ cup kim chee
½ cup hot Portuguese sausage

Chop kim chee very fine. Fry the sausage, drain and crumble as small as possible. Add to the sour cream and cottage cheese and blend well.

CHICKEN AND LUAU LEAVES (POLYNESIAN)

1¼ lb. chicken
1 cup coconut milk
1½ Tblsp. butter
1½ tsp. salt

2 Tblsp. fat
2½ cups water
6 luau (taro) leaves

Clean and cut the chicken into 1 inch cubes. Heat the fat and brown the chicken. Add 1 tsp. salt and 1 cup water and simmer until tender. Wash the taro leaves, removing the stem and tough part of the rib. Put the luau, butter, 1½ cups water and the rest of the salt in a saucepan. Simmer for one hour or until there is no sting left to the taste. Press the excess liquid from the luau, drain the chicken, combine it with the luau and add the coconut milk. Bring to the boiling point and serve immediately. Serves 6.

GREEN BEANS MACADAMIA

½ cup frozen French-style
    green beans
2 tsp. macadamia bits

1 tsp. butter or margarine
¼ tsp. lemon juice

Cook green beans according to package directions. Drain.

Meanwhile, cook macadamia bits in butter or margarine over low heat until slightly brown, stirring occasionally. Remove from heat. Stir in lemon juice. Pour butter mixture over cooked beans. Toss lightly till beans are coated. Serves 1.

SWEET-SOUR MEAT BALLS

1 lb. ground beef
1 tsp. salt
1 tsp. instant minced onion
¼ cup fine bread crumbs

1 egg, slightly beaten
⅓ cup water
1 can pineapple chunks, drained
Sweet and sour sauce

Mix first six ingredients and ½ cup pineapple chunks cut up small. Shape in small balls and set aside while making the sauce.

Sweet and sour sauce: Mix ⅔ cup each of catsup and cider vinegar with ⅓ cup brown sugar (packed). Bring to a boil.

Add meatballs and remaining pineapple chunks to sauce and simmer, covered, for about 25 minutes or until done. Serve hot in chafing dish. Makes 40 to 50 balls.

SAMOAN COCONUT CREAM

1 c. frozen coconut cream
    (thawed)

¼ c. chopped green onions
¼ c. lime juice

Mix thoroughly. Chill. To be used as a dip for cooked fish.

HAWAIIAN-STYLE BREAST OF CAPON

¾ lb. wild rice
¾ cup butter
3 whole capon breasts
   (deboned and halved)
Flour for dredging
4 cups medium white sauce
Sherry to taste
4 mushroom caps (sliced and
   sauteed in butter)
2 whole truffles (if desired
   and available, cut into
   julienne strips)
3 slices ham (sauteed in butter
   and slivered)
3 small pineapples with leaves
Sweet red pepper slices
6 fried banana halves
6 Tblsp. cooked green peas

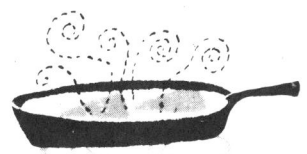

   Dredge the capon breasts in flour and cook in remaining butter turning occasionally. Cook over low heat until golden brown and cooked thoroughly.

   Cook rice and drain, melt ½ cup of the butter and, when it starts to brown, stir in the rice and remove from heat.

   Bring the white sauce to a boil and add sherry, mushrooms, truffles and ham. Keep warm.

   Split the pineapples in half lengthwise, leaving stems on. Make a cavity by removing the core and part of the pulp. Dip the pineapple shells in hot water until heated through. Drain and spoon wild rice into each half, top with chicken and cover with sauce. Garnish with red pepper slices, hot fried banana halves and cooked green peas. Serves 6.

PORK ADOBO (ADOBO BABOY) (FILIPINO)

1½ pound lean pork or
   6 pork chops
2 Tblsp. finely chopped garlic
3 bay leaves
Boiling water

6 Tblsp. vinegar
1½ tsp. salt
2 peppercorns or 1/16 tsp. black pepper

    Clean and slice pork into individual pieces for serving. Combine all the ingredients and let stand for 10 minutes in a frying pan. Add enough boiling water to cover the meat, cover the pan, and simmer until the water is evaporated. Fry the meat, adding more fat if necessary. Turn the meat to brown on both sides evenly. Serve hot.
    Chicken, fish, or beef may be prepared in the same way. Serves 6.

CHICKEN HAWAIIAN (COSMOPOLITAN)

4 boned chicken breasts
Salt and pepper
4 1-oz. pineapple spears
⅛ cup shredded coconut

1 cup flour
2 eggs
½ cup bread crumbs

    Flatten chicken breasts skin side down. Sprinkle with salt, pepper and coconut. Place pineapple spear in center of breast and roll. steam for 20 minutes. Cool.
    When cool, roll in flour, dip in beaten egg and coat with bread crumbs. Deep fry until golden brown. Serves 4.

CREPES TROPICAL (HAWAIIAN)

2 cups crushed pineapple or a
   combination of fresh
   mango, pineapple and
   banana
½ cup brown sugar (packed)

1 tsp. cinnamon
½ tsp. rum flavoring
4 dessert crepes
Sour cream
Guava jelly

    Heat ingredients, except crepes, in a saucepan. Spoon on crepes. Roll up and serve with sour cream and a dot of guava jelly. Serves 4.

MANGO CHUTNEY AND CREAM CHEESE

    Mix equal parts of chutney and cream cheese. Use as spread on crackers, toast rounds and celery or as a dip.

STUFFED CHERRY TOMATOES

Cherry tomatoes
Cream cheese
Chives
Macadamia bits

Cut off top of tomatoes and hollow out seeds. Turn upside down on paper towels to drain. Soften the cream cheese and mix it with a little mayonnaise until smooth. Add the chives, chopped fine, and macadamia bits. Fill tomatoes and arrange in a circle on plate or platter. Place parsley sprigs between them. It will look like a wreath for the holiday table.

PINEAPPLE CATAMARANS

4 small sweet potatoes
Cubed melon, watermelon, grapes or any other fruit desired
Lime sherbet or cottage cheese

Cut the pineapples the long way, leaving on the crowns (leaves). With a sharp small knife cut out the fruit in the center and cube it. In a bowl combine it with other fruits and mix lightly. Refill the shells and place a scoop of sherbet or cottage cheese on top. Serves 4.

54

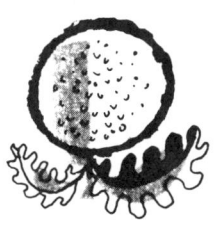

MACADAMIA CHEESE PUFFS

1 pkg. (3 oz.) cream cheese
2 Tblsp. mayonnaise
1 Tblsp. minced chives
⅛ tsp. Tabasco sauce
2 Tblsp. macadamia bits
¼ tsp. salt (omit if salted crackers are used)

Mix softened cheese with the mayonnaise. Add other ingredients and spread on crackers. Broil until light brown and bubbly. Yield: 1½ dozen.

NO-BAKE HAWAIIAN FRUIT CAKE

- 1 cup evaporated milk
- 4 cups miniature marshmallows
- 6 Tblsp. guava juice
- 8 cups fine graham cracker crumbs
- ½ tsp. cinnamon
- ½ tsp. nutmeg
- ¼ tsp. cloves
- 2 cups seedless raisins
- 1 cup dates (finely cut)
- 1½ cups macadamia nut bits
- 1½ cups mixed candied fruits (cut up)

Put milk, marshmallows and fruit juice into a 3-quart bowl. Into larger bowl, measure remaining ingredients. Work the milk mixture into dry ingredients with a spoon and then with hands until crumbs are moist. (If mixture becomes too crumbly to shape easily, add a few drops of milk.) With wet hands, fill paper baking or bon bon cups. If an icing is desired, make a thin glaze of powdered sugar and milk and drizzle over the little cakes. Sprinkle top with fresh coconut. Keep refrigerated.

What the *Bounty's* Captain Bligh needed: the ever-popular and ultra-nutritious breadfruit.

Filipino family in traditional clothing.

MACADAMIA-PINEAPPLE CHUTNEY

- 2 oz. red peppers, seeded and chopped fine (don't touch your eyes with your fingers)
- 1 fairly large bulb garlic, mashed or chopped fine
- 2 Tblsp. finely chopped fresh ginger root
- 1 Tblsp. salt
- 3 pounds peeled fresh pineapples
- 1½ pounds brown sugar
- 1½ pints vinegar
- ½ pound seedless raisins
- ¼ pounds macadamia bits

Cut the pineapple in small pieces, add the vinegar and salt and cook on low heat until tender. Add all the other ingredients and boil slowly until fairly thick, adding the nut bits last (they do not need to be cooked long). Pour into hot sterile jars and seal. May be eaten with meat, poultry or curried dishes. Yield 2 qts.

A luau in early Hawaii.

WHAT NOT TO DO — Island Style

Pity the poor cook who has never made a mistake nor learned to have fun from it. Islanders have long known there is no more nourishing dish than laughter—it's the most genuine Island-style soul food! Here are some juicy morsels dished up by the local folk; mistakes to learn from while you laugh.

YOU SHOULD NOT serve your husband salt fish as is, pouring the juice over the accompanying rice dish. If you do, you will be feeding him pure brine. Be sure the fish has been boiled in at least three waters.

YOU SHOULD NOT overdo when using shoyu. Shoyu is very salty. Use a light hand—you can always add more.

YOU SHOULD NOT serve your guests too many macadamia nuts or kukui nuts. Both have a laxative effect. Serve too many and your guests will think they have come down with a new type of Hawaiian flu.

YOU SHOULD NOT calculate one cup of raw rice per person. One cup of rice serves several—even if you have hearty appetites to feed.

YOU SHOULD NOT freeze poi. Once it's frozen, you can never redeem it. Place the bag in a bowl of water in the refrigerator, completely submerged. Then, when you mix it to the right consistency, pour it into a bowl and cover it with water so a hard crust does not form.

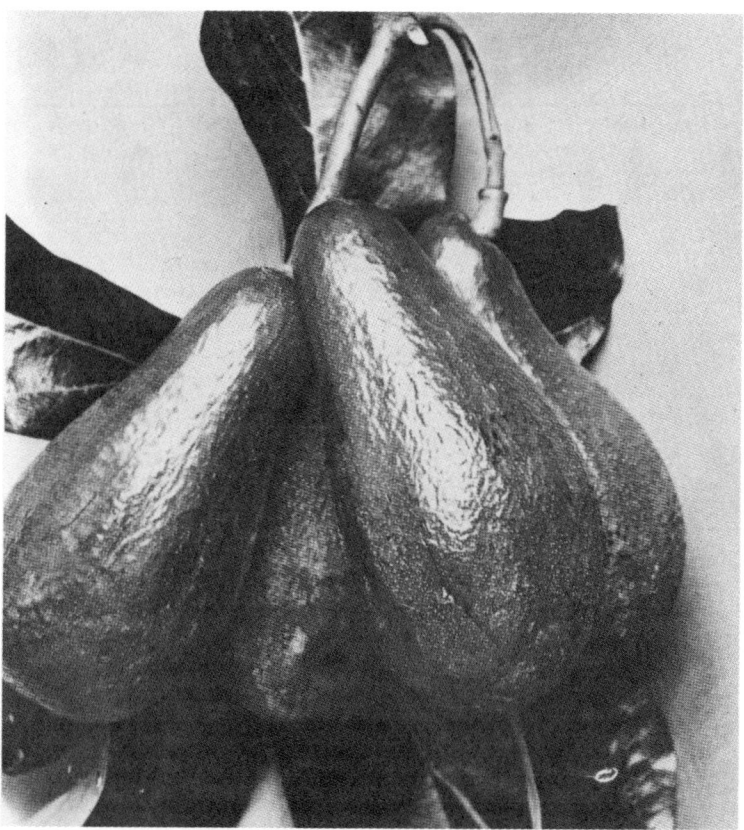

Hawaii's alligator pears make delicious eating with salads.

YOU SHOULD NOT sample champagne jelly as you go along. My neighbor made some last Christmas to give as gifts. By the time she had finished sampling and tasting each batch of jelly, she had consumed over a quart and a half. Her morning was happy but her afternoon was sick.

YOU SHOULD NOT confuse look-alikes. I took my small grandson to his first Chinese dinner. While waiting to be served, he noticed a small bowl of what he thought was butterscotch pudding in the center of the table next to the bottle of shoyu. Butterscotch pudding was his favorite and when no one was looking, he reached over and helped himself to a generous spoonful. It was hot Chinese mustard. He is older now but still not overly fond of butterscotch pudding.

YOU SHOULD NOT worry about flying bugs if you are serving outside in the summer time. On days when there is no breeze, Islanders are besieged by flying termites. They don't worry because Hawaiian termites are smart and can tell time. By 8 P.M. they have stopped swarming. Mainland bugs are probably just as smart.

A joint effort lightens the work of cooking the pig for a big luau.

"ISLANDIZING" YOUR MAINLAND DISH

1. Add finely chopped Kim Chee to meat loaf or patties.
2. Add mashed tofu to meat loaf.
3. Make a guava jelly glaze for ham or pork.
4. Add a little sake (rice wine) to stew.
5. Thicken stew with poi instead of flour.
6. Chop up Portuguese sausage in an omelet.
7. Substitute luau leaves for spinach.
8. Water chestnuts are good in a tossed green salad.
9. Add chestnuts to poultry stuffing.
10. Crush papaya seeds in an oil, vinegar dressing, tasty and healthful.
11. Make lomi salmon, drain well and serve on lettuce, as a salad.
12. Serve poha preserves over ice-cream.
13. Make a custard with coconut milk instead of regular.
14. Use sliced mangoes in a pie, following apple pie filling.
15. Add canned lychees to a fruit cocktail.
16. Combine pineapple or mango chutney with cream cheese for sandwiches.

ENTERTAINING HAWAIIAN STYLE

If a party is planned to include hot meat pupus, a variety of vegetables and chips for dipping, and sweet tidbits to round out the menu, pupus can take the place of dinner. Because hors d'oeuvres can be prepared ahead of time and frozen, refrigerated or partly cooked, the hostess has plenty of time to relax, dress and set a pretty table for a *pupu* party.

One idea for a time-saving centerpiece is an attractive fruit bowl. You can make one with a very large pineapple that has its top leaves intact. Cut the pineapple—leaves and all—lengthwise. Hollow out the fruit and cut into pieces. Return fruit to the pineapple shell with watermelon, cantaloupe and other melon balls, or with mandarin oranges, strawberries and pitted, canned lychees. Just before serving, pour two cups of champagne over the fruits. Surround pineapple with hibiscus, plumeria, orchids, and ferns for a colorful, edible centerpiece.

If possible have a second person or two in the kitchen to assist. Nothing is more disconcerting than a harried host or hostess hovering over a hot broiler or carrying trays back and forth to the serving table.

Start preparations days in advance and have your freezer clear. Freeze everything you can.

A nice touch is to provide a basket of tiny hot finger towels. Don't forget an additional dish or basket for the used towels.

We hope it won't happen, but try to be prepared for a disaster, such as a spill. Handle it as gracefully as possible and forget it.

GLOSSARY of ISLAND TERMS

Ahi	Hawaiian tuna fish	*Luau leaves*	leaves of the taro plant
Aina	Land	*Luna*	overseer
Akua	a god	*Malihini*	newcomer
Aloha	a greeting, love, affection	*Malo*	loin cloth
Aumakua	personal god	*Makai*	toward the sea
Au'au	bathe	*Mauka*	toward the mountains
Auwe	alas, oh dear!	*Mele*	song or chant
Hale	house	*Okole Maluna*	bottoms up
Haupia	coconut pudding		
Hula	Hawaiian dance	*Ono*	delicious
Imu	underground oven	*Opihi*	tiny shellfish
Inamona	relish made from crushed kukui nuts	*Pa'a kai*	salt
		Paniola	cowboy
Kalua	to bake in an underground oven	*Pau*	finished, the end
Kai	sea	*Pipi*	beef
Kamaaina	born in the Islands or old timer	*Pipikaula*	jerked or dried beef
		Poi	boiled and mashed taro root, Hawaiian staple
Kope	coffee		
Kanaka	human being (Hawaiian)	*Pua*	flower
Kapu	forbidden	*Pua'a*	pig, pork
Kukui	candlenut tree	*Puka*	hole
Laulau	pork and luau leaves wrapped in ti leaves	*Pupu*	hors d'oeuvre
		Taro	tuberous root
Lei	flowers or shell garland	*Ti*	large leafy plant
		Tempura	fried in batter
Lilikoi	passion fruit	*Tutu (or Kuku)*	grandparent
Limu	seaweed		
Lomi	massage or crush	*Ulu*	breadfruit
		Wiki or wikiwiki	hurry, quick
Luau	Hawaiian feast		

TABLE SETTING FOR A LUAU

Use any type of table, low or high, ground or floor level. Long boards laid over saw horses are suitable, or if the floor or outside ground is used, spread mats and cover with either cloth (preferably green) or tapa cloth, tapa paper, or a roll of shelf paper. Arrange ferns, flowers, or leis down the length of the table.

Pineapples may be placed at intervals. They should look whole but be cored and sliced lengthwise (a special tool is available for this) then replaced in the pineapple shell and the leafy top put back.

To create a "lagoon" for your centerpiece, a mirror may be used. Stick little mounds of sand, miniature figures of surfers, and small coconut trees (if available) on the glass. Paper dishes and napkins are perfectly acceptable but if you really want to entertain Island-style, you should set the table with washed ti leaves, since all food, except those containing a high liquid content, may be served right on the leaves. Coconut bowls add a nice Polynesian touch.

Each setting should include the following:

a dish of lomi salmon
inamona (relish made from crushed kukui nuts)
a green onion
a sweet potato in the skin
raw fish or opihi in a small dish
limu
a square of haupia

Hot dishes, as the chicken or squid luau and the kalua pig, are served after the guests are seated. Hawaiian music in the background during and after the feast is a must. So is hula dancing.

☆ ☆ ☆ ☆ ☆ ☆

☆ ☆ ☆ ☆ ☆ ☆

"ISLANDIZE" YOUR TABLE

Use all the Island touches you can manage. Sprinkle plumerias, vandas and ferns over the table. Stick toothpicks or small skewers in a whole pineapple for snack items. Provide bowls of macadamia nuts or lychees, sliced mangoes, toasted coconut strips, or colorful plates of Oriental pupus such as cubes of kanten, tiny sushi rolls or broiled rumaki.

NOTES